Animals need food and water. WomWom will look for food and water.

WomWom eats grass.
WomWom will explore what animals eat.

Some animals eat seeds as food. The hens eat seeds and grass.

Animals that eat plants and grasses are plant eaters. WomWom is a plant eater.

Cows are plant eaters too.
Cows eat plants and grasses.
WomWom can see many
cows eating in the field.

Some animals eat meat as food. A dingo only eats meat. There are no dingoes where WomWom lives.

Did you know that some birds can be meat eaters? A kookaburra eats meat. A kookaburra can catch snakes.

Animals that eat meat are called meat eaters.
A kookaburra is a meat eater.
An eagle is also a meat eater.

A dingo is a meat eater. A dingo eats animals. WomWom has to be safe from meat eaters.

Some animals eat meat and plants. Animals that eat meat and plants are called meat and plant eaters. A possum can eat insects and plants.

An emu eats plants and meat. An emu will eat insects and also plant seeds.

All animals need water to drink. WomWom will drink water. WomWom watches a wallaby drink water.